Cumann Stairiúil Cathair na Mart

– FLANAGAN'S –
HISTORY *of* WESTPORT

PEADAR Ó FLANAGÁIN BA. BComm

CATHAIR NA MART
NO. 34 · 2017

© Copyright Westport Historical Society, September 2017

ISSN 0332-4117

WESTPORT HISTORICAL SOCIETY

ADDRESS:
CLEW BAY HERITAGE CENTRE, THE QUAY, WESTPORT, CO. MAYO.

Telephone: 098 26852
Email: *westportheritage@eircom.net*
Website: *www.westportheritage.com*

PRESIDENT:
KITTY O'MALLEY-HARLOW

CHAIRPERSON:
JOHN MAYOCK

VICE-CHAIRPERSON:
AIDEN CLARKE

HON. SECRETARIES:
BRÓNACH JOYCE
DYMPNA JOYCE

HON. TREASURER:
SAL O'CONNOR

PRO:
ANNE DUFFY

COMMITTEE:
Noelene Crowe, Dominick Moran, Anna Hawkshaw, Vincent Keane, Declan Dever, Shirley Piggins, Barbara Mayock, Al Sammon, Declan Dever, Colm Cronin, Pat Warde

EDITORIAL BOARD:
Dr John Bradley, Martin Curry, Liamy McNally, James Kelly

CLEW BAY HERITAGE CENTRE LTD. BOARD OF DIRECTORS:
John Mayock, Kitty O'Malley-Harlow, Sal O'Connor. Al Sammon, James Kelly.

CONTENTS

AN OUTLINE HISTORY OF THE TOWN OF WESTPORT

PART I
**THE ORIGINS AND EARLY DEVELOPMENTS OF
THE TOWN OF WESTPORT 1750-1780** 6

PART II
WESTPORT – A NEW TOWN 1780 – 1825 14

PART III
PRE-FAMINE WESTPORT 1825-1845 22

PART IV
THE FAMINE YEARS, IT'S AFTERMATH – 1845-1855 34

PART V
**GEORGE CLENDINING – BORN IN WESTPORT 1770
DIED IN WESTPORT 1843** 40

APPENDIX 1 48
APPENDIX 2 50
BOOKS FOR SALE 115

FLANAGAN'S HISTORY OF WESTPORT

This is a reprint of articles by the late
Peadar O'Flanagáin BA. BComm. written for Cathair na Mart,
Journal of Westport Historical Society.

ADVERTISEMENT WHICH APPEARED IN FAULKNERS DUBLIN JOURNAL
17th MARCH 1767 ANNOUNCING PROPOSED NEW TOWN OF WESTPORT

TO ALL BRICKLAYERS, MASONS, STONE-CUTTERS, CARPENTERS, JOINERS, SAWYERS, SLATERS, PLASTERERS, GLAZIERS, PAINTERS, AND ALL OTHER ARTIZANS IN THE BUILDING BRANCH, AND TO THE PUBLIC IN GENERAL -

That is to inform them that a New Town is immediately to be built near the Old Town of Westport in the County of Mayo, according to plans and elevation, etc. already fixed upon, consisting of a large and elegant MARKET HOUSE, situated in the centre of an octagon area of 200 feet and to be enclosed with twelve large well finished slated houses together with three avenues for streets of thirty slated houses and several very large streets for great numbers of thatched houses and cabins to be built separately in such streets where houses, or cabins are to be admitted in at an expense from about twenty to forty guineas for each house or cabin, together with several convenient plots for cabins of inferior kind.

All workmen who are willing to contract for any of the said employments are desired to send their proposals, particularly specifying every article of their various branches in writing, sealed to the Hon. Peter Brown Kelly at Westport, Castlebar, or William Leeson, Esq., Architect, any time before 6th of April next, when their proposals will be examined and as no preference will be given to any Tradesman, it is expected all persons to whom it may be convenient, will apply, as such only will be closed with as are workmen, and willing to engage upon the cheapest terms and that can give sufficient security for the performance of their covenant. All persons who choose to take plots of ground to build upon, according to the plans and regulations for each street will meet with suitable encouragement.

Westport is situated near the sea coast, in a remarkable healthy and plentiful country, with the convenience of very fine and large lots of improvable ground, with plenty of fire and water, and several convenient plots for bleach greens, mills etc.

The plans and elevations etc. are to be seen at Westport.

AN OUTLINE HISTORY OF THE TOWN OF WESTPORT

PART I

THE ORIGINS AND EARLY DEVELOPMENTS OF THE TOWN OF WESTPORT 1750-1780

Introduction:
This article is an attempt to put into writing an outline on which a definitive history of the town can be based. The principal difficulty in attempting a definitive history at this time is the unavailability of a major archive within the town. The sources on which this article is based are therefore the printed sources presently available, together with such manuscripts sources as are available for study. The opinions reached are those of the author except where otherwise acknowledged in the text.
Westport is a comparatively recent town having developed over the past 250 years. In the present article the author will deal with the origin and early development of the new town of Westport in the period 1750-1780 and will refute some of the existing theories as to who planned the town.

Origins:
The town of Westport owes its origins to a number of factors:
1. Geographical location, sited near the mouth of the Carrowbeg River in the corner of Clew Bay at the western extremity of the central plain. The earliest habitation in the area dates back some 5,000 years and there is a variety of archaeological sites in the locality.

2. The existence of an earlier habitation site, Cathair na Mart (The Stone Fort of the Beeves), in the 16 th century an important O'Malley stronghold which was burned and destroyed by Sir Nicholas Malby, Governor of Connacht in 1583 in his campaign against the Mayo Burkes. During the 17 th century Cathair na Mart passed from the O'Malleys to Lord Mayo (Theobald of the Ships, a son of Graine Uaile), and from the 3rd Viscount Mayo to John Browne, a lawyer, who married Maud Bourke. Browne raised a regiment in the service of King James and was one of the drafters of the Treaty of Limerick. Colonel Browne settled at Cathair na Mart and built a house on or near the site of the old O'Malley fortress. He was succeeded by his son Peter to whom a curious monument exists at Carnalurgan with the inscription 'Orate Pro Anima Petri Browne Qui Fieri Fecit A.D. 1723'.

3. The character of John Browne (1709-1776) son to Peter Browne, orphaned at the

age of 15 and sent by his Protestant guardians to be educated at Oxford, from which he returned in 1729, conformed to the Established Church, and inherited the lands about Westport accumulated by his father and grandfather, which he proceeded to develop. He employed the German architect, Richard Cassels to design the present East Front of Westport House in 1732: this was executed in a simple style with cut limestone from a quarry on the Estate, and the work completed, followed by the house bridge (1734), the stable block (1735), and the old Protestant Church now in ruins in the Demesne (1736). Waterfalls were constructed in the river and the North and South Woods planted at this time.

The village of Cathair na Mart existed where the great park now lies and consisted of a High Street with alleys descending down to the river. It had a population of approx. 700 inhabitants. A small port also existed at the mouth of the river. Roads lead from the village to the west (West Road), the south (Sandy Hill Road) and the east (Old Paddock Road).

John Browne became an M.P. for the Borough of Castlebar in 1743, was created Baron Monteagle in 1760, Viscount Westport in 1768 and Earl of Altamont in 1771. By mid-century he decided on the ambitious project of building a new town on his estate, and he continued with this project until his death in 1776. It was completed by his son, Peter Browne, the 2nd Earl.

Foundation:[1]
It had been suggested that Westport was originally laid out and planned by an architect.[2] There are a number of variations on this theme:

1. The Cassels Theory - that Westport was planned by Richard Cassels in the 1730s.

2. The Wyatt Theory – that Westport was planned by James Wyatt circa 1780.

3. The French Architect Theory – that the town was planned by a French architect who came with Humbert in 1798.

   The Cassels Theory – with the exception of his designs of the East Front, Central Court of Westport House, Stable-block and Church, there does not appear to be any other plan by Cassels dating from the 1730's. The only other building dating from this period is the Old Rectory which predates the town and would possibly date from the period of the old Protestant Church, i.e. 1736.

---

[1] See Mayock, John: William Leeson, Westport's First Town Planner, Cathair na Mart, No. 18 (1988), pp 135-42.
[2] See Duffy, Fintan: Westport Estate and Town: an Example of Planned Settlement according to Picturesque Principles – Part 1, Cathair na Mart, No. 19 (1999), pp 48-64.

The Wyatt Theory – which had been quoted in many reference books, would assume a date of approximately 1780 for the town. Outside of his internal design for Westport House (1782) and those of his son Benjamin Dean Wyatt for a theatre in the town (1812) there is no evidence to support this theory.

The French Architect Theory – is more a matter of tradition and has no basis in fact. It has been found convenient to adopt a theory that would credit a particular well-known architect with the planning of the town, and in particular in the case of the Wyatt theory, this view has become generally accepted and quoted in most modern references to the town.

The question may now be asked as to who did, in fact, plan Westport. The answer is not a simple one. Westport was not planned or built in a day or, for that matter, in a year or decade. It developed over a period of more than two centuries. If any one man is to be credited with planning the town, then it must be credited to John Browne, who caused the town to be built.

We have an interesting first-hand account from this period from the pen of Dr. Pococke who visited Westport in 1752 and was a guest of John Browne. He refers to Westport (Cathair na Mart) as a village and states that Browne had decided to remove the village and to landscape the area:

> "We descended to Westport, a small village situated on a rivlet which falls into that bay, and makes the south-east corner of that great bay, in which there are some small islands.... Mr Browne's house is very pleasantly situated in the south side of the rivlet over which he has built two handsome bridges, and has formed cascades which are seen from the front of the House.....This is an exceedingly good house, the design and execution of Mr. Castles (sic): Mr. Browne designs to remove the village and make it a park improvement all round; there are fine low hills every way which are planted and grow exceedingly well; the tyde comes just up to the house and the cascades are fine salmon leaps"

Two 18 th century landscape paintings by George Moore dated 1761 at present in the Westport House collection depict the house and district from the east and from the west. In the painting from the west, Westport House is depicted as a freestanding building, alongside the Carrowbeg River with its bridges and falls. The stable-block can be seen to the left of the picture and the spire of the old Protestant Church in the background. The north and south woods and great park are in existence and there are what may well be developments in the upper right-hand side of the painting, which could represent the earliest part of the new town.

From the above-mentioned evidence I conclude that the development of the present town was commenced by John Browne between the years 1750-1760, and that the earliest developed parts of the town were along existing roads leading to old Cathair-na-Mart, Monument Street to the Fountain, the original town centre, John's Row leading to Tubberhill and thence to the West Road, and Peter Street leading to Church Street and old Cathair-na Mart. At this time the Carrowbeg River basin flowed to the North of its present course and this part of the town was developed only in later years. Bridge Street led from the Fountain to the river and Mill Street to the Old Mill that was situated under the present viaduct. The Octagon, James Street and Shop Street were developed at a later period.

Thus the early development of the town followed the natural lines of communication and the Fountain, and later the Octagon and later still the Fair Green became foci for radiating streets.

The early houses were stone-built structures; slate roofed and, for the most part, two-storey with small windows, a number of examples of which still remain on High Street, Peter Street and Bridge Street. The names of the street were either descriptive - Monument Street, High Street, Mill Street, Bridge Street or related to the Browne family- Peter Street, John's Row.

The early town was quite small as there was as yet no major industry. However this was soon introduced and the linen industry in the early 1770s was the foundation of the town's later prosperity.

The best account of this period in the town's history is that of the English traveller and agriculturist, Arthur Young, who visited Westport in the year 1776. He arrived in Westport on 29 th August:

> "In the evening reached Westport, Lord Altamont's, whose house is very beautifully situated, from a ground rising gently from a fine river, which makes two bold falls within view of his windows, and sheltered on each side by two large hanging woods, behind it has a fine view of the bay, with several headlands projecting into it, one beyond another, with two or three cultivated islands, and the while bounded by the great mountain of Crow Patrick. On the right from the hill above the house is a view of the bay and several islands, bounded by the hummolus and Clare Island with Crow Patrick rising like a superior lord of the whole country and looking down on the great region or other mountain that stretch from Joyce' Country."

His host, the Earl of Altamont, he describes as "An improver whose works deserve the closest attention". He describes the various improvements made on the estate concerned with land reclamation, application of fertiliser, rotation of crops and the introduction of the best breeds of English cattle.

He also describes the exertions made by Lord Altamont to introduce and encourage the linen industry in Westport: how he built good houses in the town which he let on reasonable terms to weavers and provided looms; and how he lent them initial capital to buy yarn, which was spun from locally grown flax, and how he encouraged the growth of a market for their produce by buying it up for the first few years;
1772 - £200;   1773- £700;   1774- £2000;   1775 - £4000.

His efforts were not in vain as buyers were attracted to the town and the market grew. He also encouraged the building of a bleach green and mill. As a result of these measures the linen industry flourished in Westport and by 1776 was producing £10,000 worth of linen, and even at that rate of manufacture they were only weaving one-tenth of the yarn spun in the neighbourhood.

The linens produced in Westport were of coarse quality and sold at from 9d. to 1/1d. per yard, the weavers earning 1d. per yard per day. The spinning of the yarn that was carried out by women and children in the home earned 2 ½d. to 3 ½d. per day. Young goes on to describe the living conditions of the people in the area. The poor live on potato for nine months of the year and bread and milk for the remainder. They have one to two cows, fish are plentiful. Menfolk fed their families from labour in the field and the family income is supplemented by the spinning of yarn by the womenfolk. Dealing with land-holdings around Westport, Young states that most of the holdings are large, from 400-500 acre stock farms, the cultivated land being sub-let at increased rents "to the oppression of the poor", who he stated "have a strong aversion to these Tierney Begs"

Rents average about 8/0d. an acre, ranging from heath-land at 2/0d. to good land at 16/0d. Ploughing is done by teams of horses, preceded by a man walking backwards in front of the horses.

The population of the area is increasing rapidly and on Lord Altamont's estate has doubled itself within 20 years. There is no emigration.

Land leases were for the duration of 3 lives or 31 years and they sold at 21 to 22 years purchase at a rack rent.

Tithes were compounded in a lump sum. Rents had fallen over the past 5 years by 13/0d. in the pound, but by 1776 were in the balance with a tendency to rise. Much of the land that was let was re-let into smallholdings.

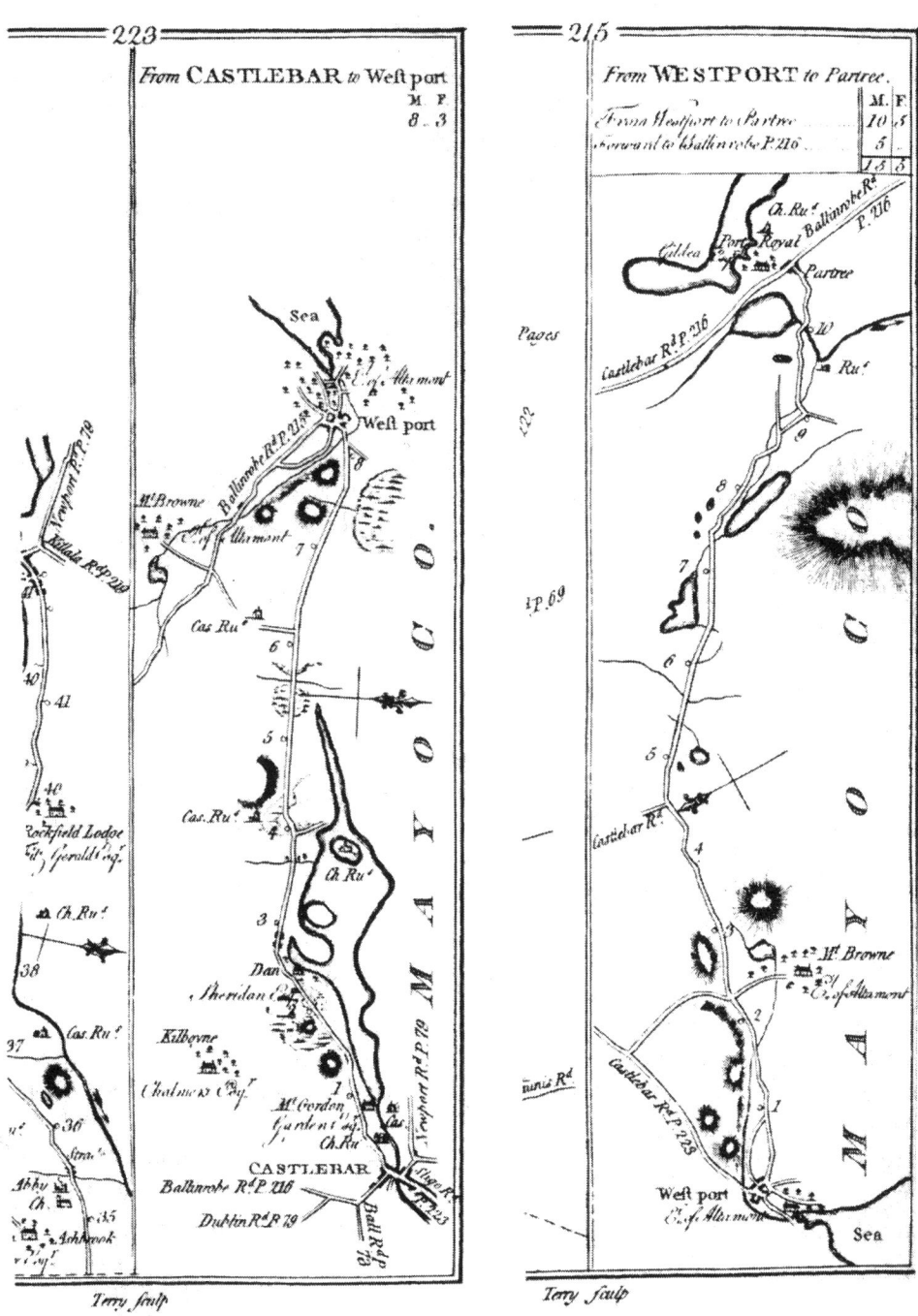

Taylor & Skinner Maps of the Roads of Ireland (1778).

From Young's detailed account, we get a picture of Westport as very much a rural town depending on agriculture as the chief industry. The introduction and development of the linen industry gave the impetus for the expansion of the town on the lines previously mentioned i.e. from the Fountain, down Bridge Street, along Mill Street, and from the Octagon down James Street and across Shop Street. The lower reaches of the town were the last to be developed.

In 1776 John Browne, 1st Earl of Altamont, died and was succeeded by his son Peter Browne as 2nd Earl, who is listed as one of the subscribers to Taylor and Skinners Maps of the roads of Ireland. This interesting publication gives us the earliest existing plan of the town (1778).

Though it is most difficult to identify individual streets, the roads leading from the town are distinguishable and it can be seen that the Carrowbeg River course has not yet been altered, and there was only one bridge over the river, across the road leading from Castlebar. There was no development north of the river.

Part of James Street, Mill Street and all of the Fair Green, Malls, Altamont Street, Castlebar Street and Newport Road had yet to be developed. The Octagon or Square as it was called may not have taken its present shape. One of the most interesting buildings in the town dating from this period is the Market House (Wyatt Theatre) with its four-arched cut-stone exterior closing the view from Shop Street. This building has been attributed to James Wyatt, but is more likely to have been designed or built, or both, by a local builder. An internal plan by Benjamin Dean Wyatt, for the theatre for the town of Westport, dated 1812 can be seen in Westport House, but his plan was not carried out.

With the death of the 2 nd Earl of Altamont in 1780, Westport was a well-established and growing town with its small port at the Quay, as yet not fully developed, its market for agriculture produce, its linen market. The only church at this date was the Church of Ireland in The Demesne; the rector was Rev. Alex Clendining. A lease for the site of the present Catholic Church had not yet been granted and Catholic services were most likely celebrated in a temporary structure at this time. The industries in the new town included milling, weaving, candle making and tanning. Agriculture, fishing and hunting would have played an important part in the local economy.

Importing, exporting and trading and manufacture would in the coming years play an even more important role in the development of the town and port in the years 1780-1820. The population, which was growing rapidly, may have been as high as 2,000 - 2,500.

The period 1780-1745 that will be dealt with in a future article was to be one of rapid growth and development during which the town and quay took the shape with which we are familiar today.

Church of Ireland in Westport Demesne.

This article was first published in ***Cathair na Mart, Vol. 1, No. 1, (1981).***

AN OUTLINE HISTORY OF THE TOWN OF WESTPORT

PART II

WESTPORT – A NEW TOWN
1780 – 1825

In my first article I dealt with the origins and early development of Westport to the date of 1780 and refuted a number of theories as to who designed the town.

In the present article I deal with the new town of Westport in a period of rapid expansion 1780 – 1825 during which the town and port took the form still familiar to us today.

The recession in the linen industry during the 1770s when the trade was first introduced in Westport was now over. The Irish Parliament became independent of Westminster and introduced freedom of trade, encouraging entrepreneurship, which led to the growth of a middle class in the towns. Leases that had been confined to a period of years, and not available to Catholics, were now expanded to leases given for three lives, which could be renewed in perpetuity. Such leases encouraged development and many of the important buildings in the town date from this period as do the vast stores that flank the quayside. These developments did not end with the Act of Union but continued well into the first half of the 19th century.

WESTPORT HOUSE AND THE BROWNES
John Denis Browne succeeded his father as 3rd Earl of Altamont in 1780.
He had previously served as M.P. for the County of Mayo. He was one of the most influential men in the County, being Lord Lieutenant of the County, Colonel of the South Mayo Militia and Leader of the Volunteers, whose flag is still to be seen in Westport House.

The 3rd Earl extended the House and commissioned the English architect James Wyatt to design the dining room and gallery. A round of festivities was held in 1783 to mark the completion of those works.

In 1778 the Lord Lieutenant of Ireland was a guest at Westport. During his stay he was taken oyster fishing in Clew Bay during which he caught a cold that was to prove fatal, as he died shortly after his return to Dublin.

Denis Browne, a brother of the 3rd Earl, lived at Mount Browne near Westport. He was elected M.P. for the county and High Sheriff of Mayo. He was later to play an infamous role in the suppression of the rebellion in 1798.

The agent of the 3rd Earl was one John Gibbons, of Drummin, who resided at Mill Street in the town. He and his family were to play an important role in the organisation of the United Irishmen in the County and to pay the price after the failure of the rebellion.

The 3rd Earl of Altamont in 1781 obtained Letters Patent from King George III granting to him the rights to hold four fairs in the town of Westport – January 1st, May 24th, August 6th and November 1st - together with the tolls and customs and a court of Pie Poudre. This Charter has recently been acquired by the local Urban District Council and historically marks the coming of age of the new town.

THE NEW TOWN AND ITS INHABITANTS
The 1780s saw the rise of a middle-class, both Catholic and Protestant, who became the principal developers of the new town and port of Westport. One of the most prominent was John Gibbons Sr., appointed c.1780 as Agent of Lord Altamont and who resided at Mill Street.

The MacDonnell and Higgins families settled in Westport at this time and were involved in commercial activities, both in the town and at Westport Quay. An inscription 'C.H. 1780' is still to be seen on James Street and 'CMD 1783' on one of the large warehouses at Westport Quay. The Levingston and Hilderbrand families also settled here at this time. The Church of Ireland rector Charles Lynagh, who in 1787 received a lease of land for the building of a Catholic Church and Presbytery, the Methodist Chapel (1791) and an Inn (1798) now Cavanaugh's Hotel. Only one bridge spanned the Carrowbeg River, connecting Bridge Street with the road to Castlebar.

In 1785 some 80 leases had been granted in the town with a total rental of £118.1.5d. The street names were as follows – Bellview (Johns Row), Bridge Street, Castle Street (Church Street), High Street, James Street, Mill Street, Monument Hill, Octagon, Peter Street, Riverside (Malls) and Shop Street.

The Principal tenants (excluding The Brownes) in town and district were: Rev A Clendining; John Gibbons Senior; Charles McDonnell; Joseph McDonnell; Charles Higgins; Patrick Clarke; Thomas Garavan; Edward Jordan; Ignatius Lynagh; Patrick McGreal; Walter O'Malley; Patrick Standford.

THE PORT AND QUAY

In 1780 Clew Bay possessed an extensive herring and oyster fishery which was responsible for first establishing the port. The corporation for the improvement of the Port of Dublin undertook developments to improve the harbour, the erection of a lighthouse and buoys and the maintenance of same until the establishment of Westport Harbour Board in 1855.

The earliest commercial enterprises were stores erected in 1783 by Charles McDonnell at the (quay) Demesne Gate. Over the next 30 years a whole range of stores and mills were erected along the quays, together with a Customs House and King's Stores, and revenue and boatmen's houses. Boffin Street was the principal residential area of the quay.

By 1818 the Quay was fully developed as a port as the following contemporary account by J.C. Curwen illustrates:

> "On inspecting the port we found a noble edifice, buildings by Messrs. Fitzgerald, as a warehouse, the scheme of which when finished is estimated at £10,000. Government is laying out large sums on improvement in the harbour. The export of grain from this port is considerable. Warm sea-water baths form a part of the sumptuous establishment of this place".

A contemporary painting by James Arthur O'Connor in the Westport House Collection, of the same date, gives a view of the quayside with the Customs House and warehouses in the background.

Westport Quays by JA O'Connor, 1818. Original painting in Westport House Collection.   Pic: © Liam Lyons

THE REBELLION OF 1798 AND ITS AFTERMATH

The influence of the French revolution of 1789 was felt even in the remote towns of the West of Ireland. It was reported to Dublin Castle that Thos. Paine's Rights of Man was on sale in the streets of Westport. During the 1790's the Society of the United Irishmen was established in Mayo and its secretary and organiser was John Gibbons Sr., Agent of Lord Altamont, who resided at Grove House on Mill Street. Gibbons was in a prominent and influential position as Agent though his militant activities were suspect by the authorities. West Mayo was one of the few areas in Connacht where the republican ideal remained alive after the brutal suppression of rebellion in the rest of the country. Lord Altamont had been instrumental in encouraging the migration of Catholics from Ulster after the battle of the Diamond in 1795. Many of those who migrated settled in the Westport district and brought with them Republican ideals. They were connected with the linen trade that flourished in this period.

When the news of Humbert's landing in Killala in August 1798 spread throughout the county, many recruits from West Mayo rallied to the cause and arrived in Castlebar after the famous 'Race of Castlebar'. Among those were John Gibbons Sr., his sons Edward and John Jr. and his brother Thomas, Westport having been surrendered to insurgents without a fight. Among those who were prominent in the leadership of the insurgents were three clergymen of the locality, Fr. Myles Prendergast of Murrisk Abbey, Fr. Michael Gannon, recently returned from France and Fr. Owen Killeen and also O'Mealy an apothecary from near Westport. James Joseph McDonnell of Carnacon, who had previously been engaged in commercial developments at Westport Quay, and was commissioned a Colonel of the Irish Forces by General Humbert, was sent, accompanied by a French Captain, to occupy and administer the town and district of Westport. The Irish Forces had already occupied Westport House and Mount Browne, and Colonel McDonnell set up his H.Q. in the former and set about establishing law and order in the locality. The occupation, however, was short-lived as Humbert moved north-eastwards towards Sligo and his final defeat at Ballinamuck. The Crown forces soon re-occupied the town, under martial law.

Among those proscribed as rebels were John Gibbons of Westport, his brother Thomas and sons, Edward and John Jr. and Fr. Myles Prendergast of Murrisk. The first three eventually escaped abroad and the latter remained as outlaws in the hills of Connemara, pursued relentlessly by Denis Browne, High Sheriff of Mayo. Browne in the early years of the 19th century was to supervise the hanging of his godson, John Gibbons, Jr. At a gallows erected at the junction of Peter Street and Tubberhill in Westport, the only person ever hanged in the town. His memory as yet unmarked in the town was relived in the poetry of the blind Raftery. The political consequence of the rebellion resulted in the Act of Union of 1800 backed by the Earl of Altamont who now became Marquess of Sligo and by his brother Denis Browne, M.P. for the county.

WESTPORT AFTER THE UNION

The Act of Union had little effect on the prosperity that Westport was to enjoy in the first quarter of the new century. The town and port continued to expand, and as far as architecture was concerned to bloom into one of the most beautiful towns in Ireland. McParlan writing in his Statistical Survey of Co. Mayo (1801) states that 'Westport, though built within 30 years, may be called a pretty and not a small town, already of some consequence in trade and expanding every day', and he refers to the export of cargoes of manganese, slates, and ochre quarried locally for the English markets. He states that a free school for the education of the poor children had recently opened in the town, that there was also the forty shilling school of the parish, and that every two or three villages had a school numerously attended. He refers to bleach mills, many oat-mills and one threshing mill, of the most improved and extensive construction on Lord Sligo's Demesne. In 1800 also Mr. Levingston opened a brewery in the town on the site of what is now the pedestrian entrance to the car park from Bridge Street. The migration of linen weavers from Co. Armagh after 1795, encouraged by Lord Altamont also helped the continued growth of the linen trade and Westport had a flourishing linen market held, probably at this period, in the Market House at the Octagon.

The newly promoted Marquess of Sligo now embarked on a very ambitious project of town planning which he must have had in mind for considerable time and which, when completed, would give to the future generations something to be proud of and to continue to conserve i.e. the Malls – a quarter mile of tree lined boulevards flanking the embanked Carrowbeg River, with two cascades, crossed by three stone-arched bridges, the whole flanked by public buildings, town houses and private dwellings with a unifying Georgian character. This project, even at that period, could not have cost less than £10,000 and possibly twice that amount. The Carrowbeg River at that time flowed to the north of its present course. It had to be canalised to flow in a straight line through the centre of the town. Even today such an operation would be a major undertaking.

There is no precise date for the Malls but, from documentation available, I conclude that a plan existed as early as the mid-1780s and that the most likely time for the construction was 1800-1810. A document in the Public Records Office, Dublin throws some light on the dating. It refers to a lease of premises in James Street to Alexander Brice, 22 October 1796, on which one house was then built. The property was re-leased by Brice to Lord Sligo, on 1st September 1807, and was subsequently leased by him to Houseman. At the end of the document was a curious detail – 'James Street now called North Mall'. The premises in question, still in the Sligo family is the corner building of the North Mall – previously known as Westport Reading Rooms – and the adjoining house on Newport Street.

An Inn was built by Lord Sligo for the use of travellers to the town, furnished by him and let at a nominal rent. This imposing building with its flanking arcaded wings, which were used for many various purposes down the years, was the centrepiece of the smaller North Mall. On the South side of the Gothic facade of the Catholic Church built in 1813 by Dr. Kelly, P.P. at a cost of £6,000 donated by public subscription, with its flanking parochial residences, equalled the buildings on the North side. Also on the South Mall there was erected in 1791 a Methodist Chapel. Bridge House at the end of North Mall would also date from this period with the present Credit Union at a later date.

The Malls were substantially finished by 1818 as can be seen from the painting by James Arthur O'Connor of this date, showing the town, looking across the Fair Green from Knockranny Hill.

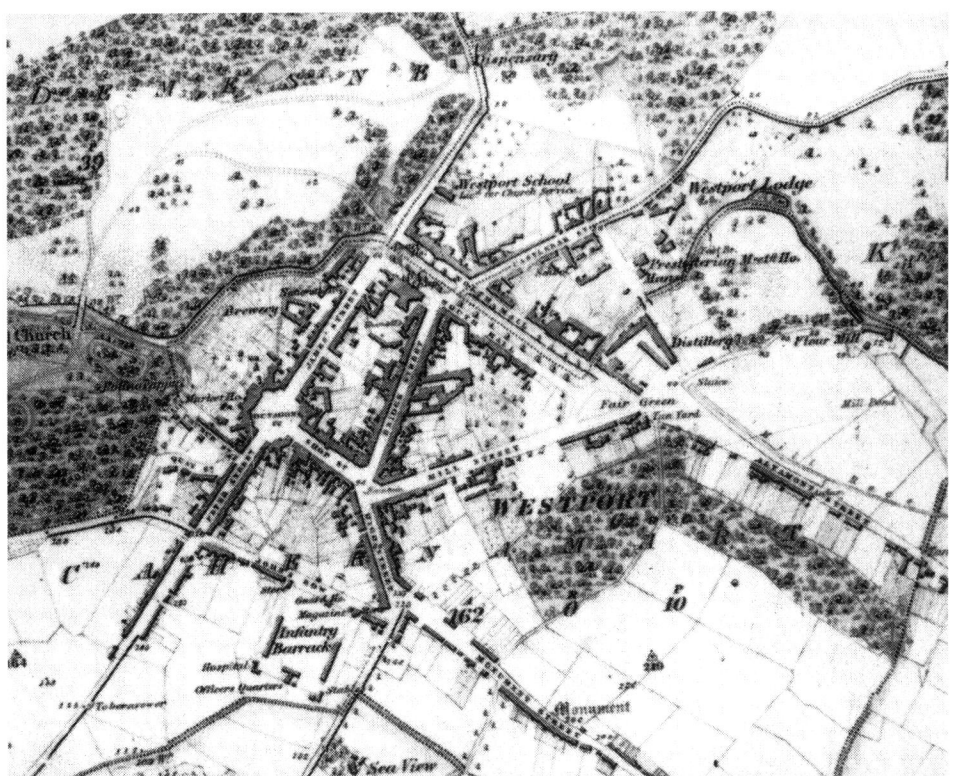

OS Map 1838. (Clew Bay Heritage Centre).

The building of the actual Mall walls and bridges was by local contractors. The western bridge (now Doris Brothers Bridge) was built by Patrick Conway who owned property on Peter Street. This would appear to be the last of the bridges built, and until recently widened by Mayo County Council, gave the impression of being unfinished on the Demesne side. At this period the entrance to Westport House was re located at the Mall, where gates and a lodge were erected, having previously been at the Paddock corner.

Castlebar Street was built also at this time leading from the centre bridge to Westport Lodge – now the Sacred Heart School – then the town residence of the Levingston family. The Malls were also linked with the Fair Green which dates from this period.

John's Row was further developed at this period when an extensive Army barracks was built there which was capable of housing five companies of Infantry.

J.C. Curwen who visited the town in 1818 states 'The plan of the town of Westport is regular and it contains many handsome houses. The Inn is on a scale suited to the most frequent place in the island exhibiting great liberality on the part of the proprietor'.

The development of the town led to an increase in population from approximately 1,000-1,785 to about 2,500-3,000 in 1815. The number of tenancies in the latter year was 230, of which the largest leaseholders were John Large £205.13s.9d; Robert Patten £197.12s.9d; Henry Patten £33.1s.3d; Colonel Browne £24.12s0d; Philip Carr £22; George Lawrence £21.4s.6d; £52.13.s.4d. was paid by the Collector of the Revenue at Foxford for the Port Surveyor's and Boatmen's Houses and £41.00 by the Collector of Tolls and Customs who occupied the Market House in the Octagon.

A visitor to Westport in 1823, T. Reid reported that:

> 'The Most Noble the Marquis of Sligo is proprietor of the town of Westport and a vast tract of coarse mountainous country in its vicinity. It is a thriving little place; the streets paved and flagged; the houses neatly built of stone and slate, from quarries of that material in the neighbourhood. It has a smart linen market, which is attended chiefly by weavers who have migrated from the County of Armagh within the last 20 or 30 years. A considerable trade in pork and oats is also carried on, but the harbour is too small and the channel too narrow and intricate for extensive commerce'.

The rapid expansion of the town led to the need for a banking service and in the year 1825 George Clendining, who was Lord Sligo's agent since 1798, was appointed as Agent of the Bank of Ireland, one of the first seven branches of the Bank outside of Dublin.

Pigot's Directory, published in the year 1824, gives us a picture of the town at the end of the period we are now examining. The Post Office was on the Mall, probably in one of the wings of the Hotel that also housed the Linen Hall and Court House, James Tayler was Post Master and Stamp Distributor, and also acted as Ships Agent and Broker and was the Magistrate's Clerk. The local Court or Petty Sessions was held weekly, and minor cases were dealt with by local magistrates or Justices of the Peace - Capt. T.D. Browne; George Clendening; Edward Fitzgerald Higgins. The Chief Constable, S. Jones, Esq., was responsible for law and order in the town. Lieutenant Irwin was in charge of the Water Guard, the predecessors of the Coast Guard. Most of the local gentry were officers of the South Mayo Militia, a force similar to the modern F.C.A. which was under the nominal command of Lord Sligo as Colonel.

James Lougheed ran a gentleman's boarding academy on the Mall. There were four apothecaries, six bakers, ten shoemakers and two breweries Levingston's and Farrell's – both on Bridge Street. There were grocers, ironmongers, leather sellers, linen and woollen drapers, painters and glaciers, saddle and harness-makers and tallow chandlers. The most numerous trade was that of the publican with a total of thirty, of who half were situated on Bridge Street.

The Dublin Mail left from the office on James Street (also known as Higgins Street) daily at 3.07am for Ballinasloe, returning to Westport at 9.50pm.

To end the period we are discussing, on November 1825, by Letters Patent, King George IV granted Market rights to Lord Sligo for the new town of Westport.

The next article in the series will deal with Westport before and after the Great Famine.

This article was first published in ***Cathair na Mart Vol. 2, No. 1, (1982).***

AN OUTLINE HISTORY OF THE TOWN OF WESTPORT

PART III
PRE-FAMINE WESTPORT 1825-1845

In previous articles I dealt with the developments of the new town of Westport in a period of rapid expansion from 1780 to 1825. In this article I propose to monitor further development in the town to the Famine times under three main headings:

Politics, Religion and Education

Trade, Commerce and Industry

Administration, Services, Law and Order.

(1) POLITICS, RELIGION AND EDUCATION
The Catholic Association founded by Daniel O'Connell had as its aim the granting of civil liberties to the Roman Catholic population who formed the great majority of the people of Ireland. It was a mass organisation with branches all over the country, even in the remote parishes of the West of Ireland. Associate members were asked to pay 1/- (one shilling) a year and the Catholic clergy who were honorary members of the Association were its chief organisers.
In Aughaval Parish the organiser was Fr. Bernard Burke who has been appointed to administer the Parish by Dr. Oliver Kelly, archbishop of Tuam, in1821. Fr Burke on his appointment had completed the church and its interior, and also built chapels at Drummin and Lecanvey, and the parochial school on Castlebar Street (1824). As organiser for the Catholic Association he was responsible for the collection of the Catholic Rent – the subscription of 1d. per month collected at the chapel door, which went towards the expenses of the Catholic Association. The movement grew in the years 1826-1829 into a mass organisation under the leadership of O'Connell. Following a number of abortive Emancipation Acts, O'Connell who was a Roman Catholic, and thus debarred from taking a seat in the House of Commons, was persuaded to stand for Clare in the by-election of 1828. He had the full support of the Catholic Association and won a resounding victory, the result of which was the passing of the Catholic Emancipation Acts of 1829 granting to Roman Catholics the right to sit in Parliament and to all but the highest offices.

The granting of Emancipation was celebrated by the lighting of bonfires and the erection of commemorative crosses, one of which remains to this day at Thornhill erected by the McDonnell family. The campaign for Emancipation also introduced the priest into politics as the clergy were foremost in organising the people at local level.

Those who lost out were the forty shilling freeholders who were disfranchised by the Act, the new qualification being the £10 freehold.
The commission of Public Instruction gives the following statistics regarding religious denominations in Aughaval parish in 1831 and 1834 respectively:

Established Church 633-483

Catholic Church 13,193-14,358

Presbyterian 17-58

Methodists 78-53

The Parish Church (Established) was situated in the Demesne and was attended weekly by approximately 300. There was a non-resident Vicar and three curates. Approximately 3,000-4,000 weekly attended the Roman Catholic chapel, situated on the Mall. There was Mass twice on Sundays and Holidays and one on weekdays. There was a non-resident Parish Priest, a resident Administrator and three curates.

A Presbyterian House had recently been built at Distillery Road (Kirk Lane) and a resident minister conducted service to 34-40 parishioners twice on Sundays and once on Friday evenings.

There was a Wesleyan Methodist Meeting House on the Mall in which a resident minister conducted service three times on Sunday and twice each weekday for approximately 80-100 parishioners.

A male and female national school was conducted at Castlebar Street under Mr. and Mrs. Harrow, Master and Mistress, who were paid partly by the Board and partly by local subscribers. There were 236 males and 103 females on the rolls. The female school had recently closed because of lack of local subscription.

A male and female free school under the Kildare Street and Tuam Diocesan Societies were lodged in a new building in the Newport Road (now known as the Lecture Hall). This building had been converted into a fever hospital at the time of the cholera epidemic of 1831 and subsequently the upper story of the building, built by public subscription, was consecrated for Protestant service. These schools were run by Mr. and Mrs. Jas. Daly who received a grant from the Society together with

Westport House

local subscriptions. There were a total of 79 on the rolls. In the town of Westport there were also quite a number of private schools with numbers varying from 13 to 100, payment being made quarterly by the children, and also an Infant School conducted by Samuel Flynn and Susan Wilkes with 43 on the rolls, £23 per annum paid by local subscription.

The years after the granting of Catholic Emancipation until the death of O'Connell in Genoa saw the second great popular movement led by the Liberator – The Repeal of the Act of Union. O'Connell was now a figure of European importance and the undisputed leader of the Irish people.

Inglis refers to the absence of Lord Sligo from Westport during this period when he became Governor of Jamaica and to the results of O'Connell's emancipation of the Roman Catholics:

"Good and bad men have alike been driven from the representation of counties and boroughs in Ireland, by agitation; but in all cases – in cases where the people were wrong, as well as in those where they were right, they were originally mere tools in the hands of the resident working agitators - the priests - who were themselves tools in the hands of the absentee master agitator. Some change has now taken place in this. O'Connell does not work now, so much through the medium of priests, as directly upon the people by epistles and speeches, and my persuasion is that the fiats of O'Connell would be obeyed, even if the priesthood opposed them. I believe it frequently happens now and will happen still more frequently, that it is the priests who, through self-interest, find it necessary to move with the people – not the people who are incited to agitation by the priests. This I know to be the opinion of several of the more respectable Catholic dignitaries, who are opposed to O'Connell and agitation."

The year 1843 saw the peak of the Repeal agitation when O'Connell organised the Irish people as they had never been organised before by means of monster meetings at which over 100,000 people attended – one such meeting was held outside Westport on the top of Sheeaun.[1] The government defeated the agitation by using coercion. O'Connell died on the eve of the famine and on his journey to Rome, of a broken heart.

Before his death Dr. Oliver Kelly, Archbishop of Tuam, had secured for his friend, Dean Bernard Burke, a papal brief appointing him Parish Priest of Westport (Aughaval). The Dean was also the first named on the list of clergy of the diocese to succeed Dr. Kelly, but the bishops of the province favoured one of their numbers, Dr. McHale, who was appointed. Dr. McHale promptly appointed the Dean to the rural parish of Kilmeena, and on this first visitation to Westport was welcomed by the Dean and parishioners, only to be told privately by the Dean of this appointment to the parish of Westport. McHale attempted without success to question the brief appointment but Rome held in favour of the Dean who was to be the last resident Parish Priest of Westport.

In the Church of Ireland (Established Church) the position was similar in that a Vicar of Westport had been non-resident. In 1836 Archdeacon Grace resigned his incumbency and Rev. Patrick Pounden was appointed Vicar. The Vicar paid rent to Lord Sligo for the Glebe land and there was also a charge on the Glebe house to the Boards of First Fruits for money advances for its building. He also paid rent of the schoolhouse.

---

[1] *There is a longstanding tradition in Westport that this meeting occurred. I can find no evidence for it. O'Connell did hold an indoor meeting in Westport. (Ed.)*

The English novelist, W. M. Thackeray, describes a Sunday in Westport during a visit in 1840:

> "The chapel is before the Inn where I resided, and on Sunday from a very early hour, the side of the street was thronged with worshippers, who came to attend various services. Nor are the Catholics the only devout people of this remote district. There is a large Presbyterian church very well attended, as was the Established church service in the pretty church in the park. There was no organ but the clerk and a choir of children sang hymns sweetly and truly; and a charity sermon being preached for the benefit of the Diocesan Schools. I saw many pound notes in the plate, showing that the Protestants here were as ardent as their Roman Catholic brethren."

Unhappy with the running of the National Schools and desirous of having an order of nuns in the parish, Dean Burke applied in 1841 to Mother McCauley, foundress of the Sisters of Mercy, to found a house in Westport. In 1842 three sisters were sent form Carlow under Sr. Mary Paul Cullen (a sister if Cardinal Cullen). The sisters were put up at first in the Dean's own house on the Mall, while the convent was under construction on a site donated by Lord Sligo at Altamont Street. Dean Burke himself contributed £200 and set about the task of fund-raising for the balance of £3,000 throughout Ireland and England. The sisters first occupied the convent in 1843 and the schools were occupied in 1845. The small community took on new recruits locally and were given charge of the parochial schools, at first on Castlebar Street and later at Altamont Street.

(2) TRADE, COMMERCE AND INDUSTRY

The trade of Westport Quay consisted of the export of agricultural produce, and the import of timber from America and the Baltic and British manufactured goods. In 1834, 116,117 quarters of grain and 5,410cwts. of flour and meal were exported to British ports. The number of registered vessels amounted to six, some 101 ships entered the port and 153 cleared the port that year. A herring fishery existed, though not as extensive as in former years.

In the town Wm. Levingston founded an extensive distillery in 1826, which produced annually 60,000 gallons of whiskey and consumed 29,000 bushels of grain. The distillery, which was situated at what is now called Distillery Road, was water-powered by means of a mill-race from the Carrowbeg River which ran down one side of Altamont Street, where the Convent Primary School is now situated. The brewing business of Levingstons on Bridge Street was in decline at this time, because of the reduction of the tax on spirits. The Levingstons employed some 150 people on a regular basis.

A second brewery and malting concern was run by Messrs. Graham together with two salt-works and three corn stores at the Quay, and a tannery in the town, giving employment to some 30 people in summer and 60 in winter. The Manor flour and oat mills, which were built by Lord Sligo in 1808 situated near the present railway viaduct, were water driven by two wheels with 30 horse power.

At Cloonagh were the extensive flourmills of Messrs. McDonnell and Whittle, the ruins of which can still be seen – they were water-powered from the Belclare River. The McDonnell's also had a corn and flourmill at the Quay. At Belclare was a cotton factory of 26 looms employing 30 men and also women and children. There was also a bleach-green and a linen and cotton manufacturing industry of Messrs. Pinkerton and Thompson of 24 looms, producing weekly 48 webs of 52yds.each, giving regular employment to 50 and up to 200 when in full operation. At this time, however, there was a marked decline in the important linen market, as reported by H.D. Inglis during his visit here in 1834:

"Westport was once a very flourishing town. The linen trade was extensively carried our there, and 8 years ago, as many as 900 pieces were measured and sold on market-day. Now the quantity scarcely averages 100 pieces. Taking the whole district, including Westport, Castlebar, Newport-Pratt, Ballinrobe and the immediate country, about 500 pieces are sold weekly, and about 30,000 are supposed to be, less or more, employed in the trade. No trade gives such universal employment as this. Not fewer that 60 persons are employed, from first to last, in preparing a web of linen.

The linen trade in this district, and probably in other districts, is the source of all the extras that are obtained beyond the absolute necessities of life.
The land is let in very small portions: 7 or 8 acres is about the usual size of a 'take'. Potatoes are raised for the family consumption, grain to pay the rent; and the flax is destined for clothing and extras. The decline of the linen trade had produced great want of employment; and the condition of the agriculturists throughout these districts have very much deteriorated."

Of the Quay he reports:
"Westport possesses a considerable export trade in grain. About 15,000 tons are exported, of which the largest portion is oats; the next barley; and the smallest portion, wheat. There are extensive corn stores at the quay; and the harbour is good and secure."

Inglis happened to be in Westport on a Thursday that, then as now, was a market day. He gives an interesting account:
"The town had an appearance of considerable business; but with the exception of manufactured linen, this appearance was deceptive. It is true, there were many people on the market and much buying and selling; but the articles

brought to market were in most cases of very trifling value. I saw hundreds of women, standing with but a few hanks of linen yarn worth a shilling or two; hundreds with an apron full of wool, worth much less. Some of these bundles of wool, indeed, were the shearings of one or two sheep, the property of the farmer's wife or daughter, and were sent to be converted into ribbons or gloves, but notwithstanding these exceptions, it is certain that there is much evidence of the poverty of the surrounding country, in the small value of the articles to market and in the great distance they are carried. I know of 3, 2 and even 1 egg, being brought to Westport from a distance of 2 miles. I saw a girl take her seat in the market with 5 eggs worth 11/2 d. and she walked as much as a mile and a half to bring these to market."

W.M Thackeray writes of the dying trade at Westport Quay in 1840, in his Irish Sketch Book:

"There was a long handsome pier (which, no doubt, remains at this present minute), and one solitary cutter lying alongside it which may or may not be there now. There were about three boats lying near the cutter, and six sailors, with long shadows, lolling about the pier. As for the warehouses they are enormous; and might accommodate, I should think, not only the trade of Westport, but Manchester too. There are huge streets of these houses, ten storeys high, with cranes, owners' names, etc., marked Wine Stores, Flour Stores, Bonded Tobacco Warehouses, and so forth. The six sailors that were singing on the pier no doubt are each admirals of as many fleets of a hundred sail that bring wines and tobacco from all quarters of the world to fill these enormous warehouses. These dismal mausoleums, as vast as pyramids, are the places where the dead trade of Westport lies buried – a trade that, in its lifetime, probably was about as big as a mouse. Nor is this the first, nor the hundredth place to be seen in this country, which sanguine builders have erected to accommodate an imaginary commerce. Mill owners over mill themselves, squires over castle themselves, little tradesmen about Dublin and the cities over villa and over gig themselves, and we hear sad tales about hereditary bondage, and the accursed tyranny of England".

However, the statistics of the same period tell a different tale. On 31 December 1843 there were four sailing vessels (aggregate tonnage, 83 tons) registered at the port. During that year, 73 ships entered the harbour and 151 sailed from the harbour coast-wise. Two ships entered from the colonies and are sailed to the colonies. During 1835, the exports amounted to £87,805, consisting of 292,485 cwts. of corn, meal and flour, 1,061 cwts. of provisions, 5,561 gallons of spirits, 11 bales of wool, 7 bales of linen, and 77 bales of flax and tow. Imports in 1835 amounted to £28,517 consisting of 2,533 tons pf coal, calum and cinders, 250 tons of iron, 30 tons of cast-iron, 20 tons of lead, 166 tons of slates and stones, 1,400 tons of salt, 2,878 cwts. of corn ,meal and flour, 165 cwts of ashes, 3,200 cwts. Of potatoes, 284 cwts of barilla, 128 pieces of sugar, 1,759 tons of flax seed, 138 casks of tallow, 509 barrels of herrings, 11,172 gallons of spirits and 260 packages of glass earthenware. The estimated amount of inland carriage to the town consists of 14,000 tons of exportation, 3,375 tons of agricultural produce for local consumption as food, 1,000 tons of agricultural produce for the use of breweries and distilleries, 50 tons of excisable articles not received by direct importation and 7,000 tons of stone, lime, turf, and other heavy and bulky articles, and the estimated amount of inland carriage from the town consists of 1,860 tons of coal, manure and other heavy and bulky articles.

As can be seen Westport was an important entrepôt port for a large inland region. Jonathan Binns, an Assistant Agricultural Commissioner on the Irish Poor Inquiry visited Westport, and in his account "The Miseries and Beauties of Ireland" (1837) reports on the spirit trade:

"The town of Westport contains about 4,500 inhabitants, 400 houses and 53 licensed public houses or spirit shops – so that there is rather more than one spirit shop to every 8 houses. In the rest of the barony, with a rural population of nearly 30,000 there are but 6 licensed spirit houses, a less number than formerly. The increase of the licensed spirit shops has been considerably checked of late by the refusal of the magistrates to grant licences, but over the unlicensed houses, which very in number as the seasons are good or bad, they cannot of course exercise any control. When the oat crop has been plentiful, the price of grain is proportionately low; a large portion of it is secretly malted and distilled. In this way, it yields more than if sold in the market in its raw state; and under these circumstances, the unlicensed houses frequently exceed in number those that are licensed.

Notwithstanding these facts, the people are a sober people. It was remarked in evidence that in most places 'they were more hungry than drunk'."

(3) ADMINISTRATION, SERVICES, LAW AND ORDER

Under King George IV, 15 Town Commissioners were elected to oversee the paving of the streets, town lighting and the watch. No records of the Commissioners appear to be extant. In 1831 the town contained 617 houses and 4,448 inhabitants. There were four fairs held each year and the market day was Thursday.

The town had a Market House on the Octagon and a Linen Hall on the Malls.

The town contained one hotel – Robinson's on the Mall (now Cavanaugh's), which was greatly praised by visitors to the town. The hotel that was built and furnished by the first Marquess of Sligo was let rent free to the landlords, Mr. and Mrs. Robinson, provided they maintained a service for the visitors to the town. In

Market House (Artwork by Pamela Gray).

addition to Robinson's Hotel on the Mall, there was the Eagle Hotel run by Mary Walsh on Castlebar Street.

A branch of the Bank of Ireland had been established since 1825 and was situated on Mill Street. Messrs. Alexander and George Clendening were joint Agents, and Mr. Stephen William Dudgeon was Manager of the recently established National Bank of Ireland (founded by O'Connell) in Higgins Street (now James' Street).

The post office was situated on High Street (in the premises presently owned by Miss McGing) and Miss Elizabeth Hildebrand was the postmistress. There was a news room on the Mall.

Westport was also the head of a coastguard district with out-stations at Innisturk, Old Head, Islandmore, Mynish, Achill Beg and Killeen. The force of 6 officers and 52 men was under a resident inspecting Commander.

The military barracks was situated above the town at John's Row (Barrack Street) and had accommodation for 5 companies of infantry (both regular and militia). This was also the H.Q. of the local South Mayo Militia. J. J. Lovelock was Barrack Master.

The General Sessions for the county were held in the newly constructed courthouse at Castlebar Street in April and October (the equivalent of our Circuit Court) and Petty Sessions were held every Thursday, attended by the local magistrates or justices of the peace (the equivalent of our District Court). A manorial court for small claims under £10 Irish was held on the last Friday of every month. John Large was keeper of the Courthouse and Bridewell.

Inglis gives us an account of the Petty Sessions that he attended in 1834:

"I attended a Petty Sessions at Westport and found a good deal to interest me. The classes of cases were the same as I had already seen elsewhere; but there was some little difference in the character of the assault cases, which were of a less barbarous kind than those I have seen tried at the Tralee sessions. Here, also, were more cases of larceny, which had been very rare further south. I found at Westport the same contempt of truth, the same disregard of an oath, the same clanship as I had found elsewhere.

Most of the cases tried originated in the competition for, or possession of, land. Many were cases of trespassing; many cases in which the driving of cattle to the pound created contentions and outrage; and some, cases of disputed possession of land and houses, which had been the cause of outrage. The Clerk of the Sessions informed me that the criminal business had greatly increased since the decline of the linen trade; and that it rarely happened that those in full employment were implicated in any matter requiring magisterial interference. I saw less formality and more of the free and easy at the session here, than I had seen elsewhere. Everyone took a hand in what was going on, Lord Sligo's driver who was sitting near, would say of a witness 'Don't believe it, your Worship', and a clerk, an interpreter, or even a reporter for a newspaper would suggest a question, and the magistrates would interrogate accordingly."

The Irish Poor Law Act 1838 set up the Poor Law Board (the predecessor of the modern Health Boards) that divided the country into a number of Unions based on the major towns with their hinterlands. Westport was selected as the centre of the Union that covered some of the most remote areas of the country stretching from the Killaries to Ballycroy. It was declared on 13th July 1840, comprising an area of 341,117 acres with a population (1831) of 77,512 with the following divisions: Westport 15,315. Lewisburgh 9,718, Clare Island 3,632, Aughower 12,025, Clogher 4,417, Kilmeena 9,000, Kilmaclasser 3.444, Newport 11,761, Achill 5,277, Ballycroy 2,925. There were 8 ex-officio and 26 elected guardians of which 5 were elected for the Westport Electoral District. The Unions were to be financed by the Poor Rate, a rate on property that remains to the present day. A workhouse was erected in the principal town of each Union. The Westport workhouse was contracted for on 29th Oct. 1840, on a site belonging to Lord Sligo at Cahernamart where the present U.D.C. housing scheme exists. The site of some 7 acres was subject to a ground rent of £14.3s.6d., a matter of contention up to the present time. The workhouse was designed to a common plan for such buildings and for the accommodation of 1,000 paupers. The cost was estimated at £7,800 for the building, etc., and £2,000 for the site, etc. The total cost to the Union by 6th of February 1843, at which date the workhouse was not open for the reception of paupers, was £1,612. The balance was met by a loan from the Poor Law Board.

The Westport guardians held their meeting in August 1840 under the chairmanship of Lord Sligo. They borrowed £9,800 to finance the workhouse and the building was finished two years later and was seen by W.M. Thackeray, the novelist, on his visit to Westport in that year:

> "Hard by was a large Gothic building – it is but a poorhouse; but it looked like a grand castle in the grey evening."

That year the building was declared fit for the reception of paupers by the Board but because of the difficulty in collecting the poor rate to finance the running of the Union, remained closed.

In 1843 the following were elected for the Westport Electoral District: Marquess of Sligo, Westport House; Charles F. Higgins, Trafalgar Lodge; William Levingstone; H. W. Mc Ilree; William Graham; of Westport.

For Louisburgh Electoral District: George Clendening, Westport; Redmond Lyons, Accony; John Gibbons, Clooncura.

For Aughower electoral District: Dominick Kearns and Patrick Gallagher of Westport.

Mr. Joe Roe was Master of the workhouse.

The difficulty of collecting the poor rate remained, and in 1844 a warship and two revenue cruisers were dispatched to Clew Bay, and the rate collectors has the assistance of 2 companies of the 69th Regiment, and a troop of the 10th Hussars, together with 2 magistrates, two police inspectors and 50 constables to help in the collection of the rate; a situation which led to questions in the House of Commons. The workhouse remained closed and in debt. The Board of Guardians resigned in October 1844 and a new board was elected. Finally in June 1845, a writ of Mandamus was issued against the Board, forcing them to open their doors on the 8th November of that year. Under the Poor Law Guardians a dispensary was set up in Westport for the town and district with a resident medical officer. The dispensary served an area of 77,927 acres with a population of 26,345 and in 1840/1 it expended £169.0s.1d and administered to 1,450 patients. By 1844 the dispensary administered outdoor relief to 7,400 of the poor, a great number of whom were visited by the medical officer in their homes. Dr. Thomas Hamilton Burke was the dispensary doctor.

The population of the town in 1841 (the last census prior to the Famine) was 4.912 which included Westport Quay (547).

The Royal Mail Coach left from the Royal Mail Coach Office on the South Mall (beside Methodist church) and from Robinson's Hotel, every morning at 3a.m. travelling via Castlebar, Ballinrobe, Tuam and Athlone, to Dublin. A car left each morning at 5.00 a.m. from Shop Street to Ballinasloe, meeting the Grand Canal Boat to Dublin. A mail-car left the Royal Mail Coach Office at 5.30 a.m. each morning to Castlebar, connecting with the Sligo Royal Mail. The 'Shareholders Car' left Robinson's Hotel at 7.30 a.m. each morning for Galway. A mail-car left from Peter Street each day at 4.00p.m. for Louisburgh and a car left Bridge Street each day at 4.00 p.m. for Newport.

Thus we see further growth in Westport in the first half of the 19th century. However, there were signs already appearing of the terrible calamity that awaited the people, the famine.

Sources:
H.D. Inglis, A Journey throughout Ireland, 1834.
Jonathan Binns, The Miseries and Beauties of Ireland, 1837.
W.M. Thackeray, Irish Sketch Book, 1862.
Lewis, Topographical Dictionary of Ireland, 1837.
Parliamentary Gazetteer of Ireland, 1845.
Slater's Directory, 1846.

This article first appeared in ***Cathair na Mart No. 3. (1983).***

AN OUTLINE HISTORY OF THE TOWN OF WESTPORT

PART IV

THE FAMINE YEARS, IT'S AFTERMATH – 1845-1855

In my last article, I outlined the development of the Irish Poor Law in the years leading up to the Famine. Westport was the administrative centre for the Westport Poor Law Union, covering the coastal area between Killary Harbour and Blacksod Bay, and the site of the Union Workhouse, situated at Cahernamart, where the Board of Union, ex officio and elected members, held their meetings. It was only opened on the eve of the Famine by Mandamus order of the courts. In the present article, I deal with the town of Westport during the Famine years.

The commissioners enquiring into the State of the Poor in Ireland in the years immediately preceding the Famine give a picture, drawn Parish by Parish, of a rapidly increasing population steeped in poverty with little future prospects. The Parish of Oughoval (Aghavale), which includes the town of Westport, was no exception and the respondents to the Commissioners' queries, mostly clergymen of the various denominations, refer to the poverty of the people in general, begging for money in the streets if the town, or for food in the country areas; over-crowding in the town, with from 2 to 8 families occupying the same house and a large number of lodgings with nightly rates varying from ½d. to 2d.; a rapidly expanding population, whose condition had continued to deteriorate since the peace of 1815. Since that date also, with the exception of faction fights, there was little violence in the parish. Though many existed at subsistence level there had be no reported deaths from starvation. The potato was the staple food of the vast majority of the Irish people, and when this was struck by disease, famine inevitably resulted. The disease struck in autumn 1845 and the reaction of the Government was to set up a Relief Commission to supervise the alleviation of the distress. The commission had four means of doing this:

1. At local level relief committees would be set up to raise subscriptions and to buy food. The funds locally raised would be equalled £ by £ by the Commissioners.

2. Public works were to be commenced so that the able bodied would have sufficient money to buy food. The public works were to be supervised by officials of the Board of Works.

3. In anticipation of the fever that would follow the famine each Board of Guardians was to erect a fever hospital adjacent to the workhouse.

4. The Government was to expend £100,000 on the purchase of Indian meal in the United States, which would be stored at depots under Commissary officers, and used to lower the market price of grain as necessary.

The potato disease if 1845 was only partial and it was not until 1846, when the potato crop failed totally, that the plight of the Irish people became known generally and large and massive relief measures were undertaken both by the Government, the British Association and the Society of Friends.

The Society of Friends (Quakers) in response to the great distress in Ireland established a Central Relief Committee in Dublin and sent William Forster as their agent to Westport in 1846. His son William Edward Forster joined him on 18th January 1847. The latter describes the state of Westport at that time.

'.... The town of Westport was in itself a strange and fearful sight. Like what we read of in beleaguered cities, its streets crowded with gaunt wanderers sauntering to and fro with hopeless air and hunger-struck look; a mob of starved, almost naked women around the poor house, clambering for soup tickets; our Inn, the headquarters of the road engineer and pay clerks, beset by a crowd of beggars for work.'

On 1st January 1847 the British Association appointed Count Strzelecki, a Polish noble as their agent in the North West of Ireland, and he left immediately for Westport, from where he reported:

'.... No pen can describe the distress by which I am surrounded, you may now believe anything which you hear and read, because what I actually see surpasses what I ever read of past and present calamities.'

Both the Central Committee of the Society of Friends and the British Association approved grants which were disbursed though the local Relief Committees which hade been set up, including Westport Relief Committee.

A Committee for the relief of distress was formed in Westport on 16th December 1846, consisting of nine members. The committee within the first month had raised a sum of £232.14s.0d and in January 1847 amalgamated with a number of smaller committees in the district who were represented by a further nine members, making a total of eighteen.

By 2nd of February the amount raised was £721. 14s.7d. and application was made to the Relief Commissioners for an equal sum to be added to their funds.

A Committee's function was to co-ordinate the various relief measures in their area and to submit lists of the distressed. The Committee membership was representative of the local landlords, merchants and religious of the various denominations. The secretary of the Committee was the Rev. Patrick Pounden, Vicar of Westport, who corresponded with the Relief Commissioners in Dublin. They met regularly in a room in the town known as the Relief Committee Room. They also co-ordinated the relief measures sponsored by both the British Association and the Central Committee of the Society of Friends whose agents Mr. Wm. Forster and Count Strzelecki visited Westport in the winter of 1846-47.

The activities of the expanded relief Committee were wound up at a meeting held at Westport Courthouse on Thursday, 16th September 1847, the Most Noble the Marquess of Sligo in the Chair.

It was moved by Robert Buchanan, Esq., J.P. of Prospect and seconded by Rev. Thomas O'Dowd, R.C.C. and resolved:
> '... That the proceedings of the several committees in the Union being now brought to a close, we cannot separate without conveying to the British Association our warmest thanks for the aid which they have given us during the awful visitation with which it has pleased the Lord to visit us. They came to our aid at a period when thousands of persons would unavoidable have fallen victims to famine and disease, and while wants of the destitute were this provided for, an additional obligation was conferred upon us by the maintenance of our juvenile population in the several schools which were enabled to keep open and thereby not alone relieve their physical wants, but extend the blessings of education so necessary for the well-being of society. Their kindness was much enhanced by the funds having being disbursed by the hands of Count Strzelecki whose urbane and courteous demeanour and anxiety for the destitute deserving of our heartfelt gratitude.'

The Secretary of the Committee at this time, George Hildebrand, forwarded the above resolution to the British Association in London, to Count Strzelecki in Dublin and had same published in the daily and local papers..

Opened on 5th November 1845 for the reception for the destitute poor the Workhouse at Cahernamart was, during the following five years, to be the only hope of refuge for those who could no longer survive on the land. The large building was capable of housing 1,000 men, women and children and segregation of the sexes was strictly enforced.

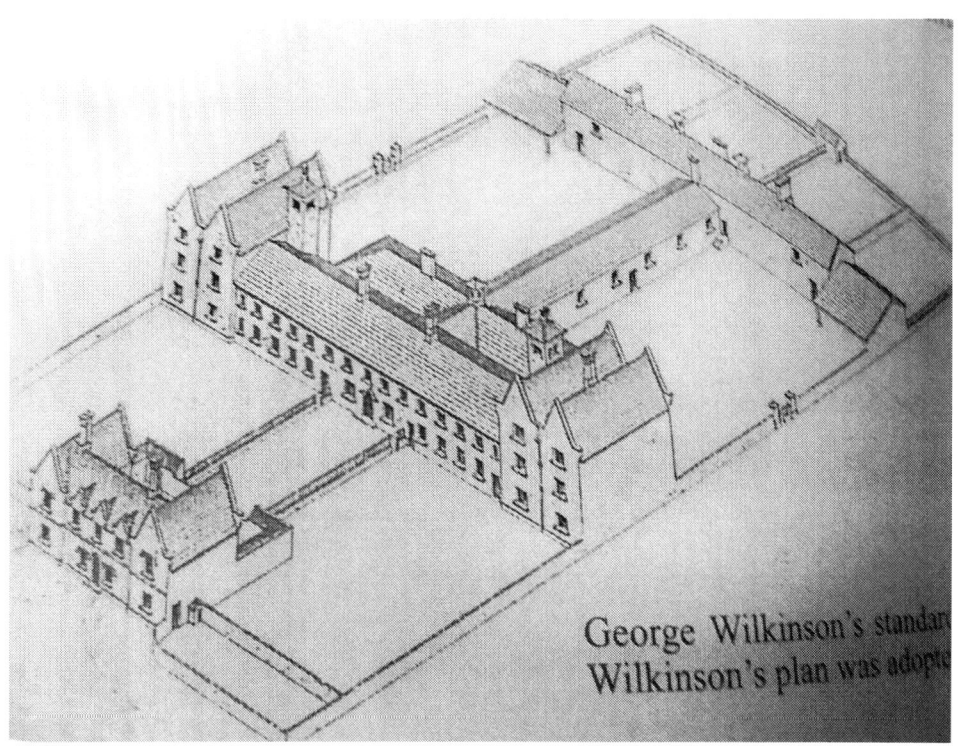

Most Workhouses in Ireland were built to a standard plan by George Wilkinson.

The Poor Law Guardians met in the Boardroom above the Gate Lodge once a week to discuss the affairs of the Union and the running of the Workhouse. The clerk of the Board was John Large. At their meeting of 27th June 1846 the uncollected rates totalled £840.17s.43/4d. of which sum €116.0s.03/4d. was in respect of the Westport area. On 11th July 1846 it was resolved that stirabout be substituted for potatoes at dinner for the next week. By August 1847 £800 was owed by the Westport Guardians, £1,000 was due in repayment of the erection loan and no rates were coming in. New Guardians were elected on 29th September 1847 including the Marquess of Sligo (Chairman), James Hileas – Maryland, Sir Richard O'Donel (Vice-Chairman), Dominick J. Bourke-Greenhills, Fitzgerald Higgins, G.G. Higgins, G. Clendining, M. MacDonnell- the last four were from Westport. By early December there were 600 inmates, and as only £62 in rates had been collected, there was insufficient money to feed them. Mr George Hildebrand, a local merchant, donated £60 towards the cost of food. At their meeting of 16th December the Guardians proposed that a rate be levied on the electoral divisions of the Union and that 1/3d. in the £ be the highest rate, each electoral division to be levied in proportion to its expenses.

At the meetings of 14th and 20th January, the Guardians sent desperate appeals for help to the Poor Law Commissioners. Mr Hildebrand's £60 had been used up and the Chairman Lord Sligo agreed to maintain the Poorhouse at his own expense for a further three weeks "rather than that the unhappy occupants should be expelled." Matters did not improve, however and the Guardians found it more difficult to raise funds. At their meeting of 25th March, George Clendening, Esq. was elected Deputy Vice-Chairman and a Finance Committee was appointed consisting of: Joseph A. Burke, William Grant, Pat Sheridan and George Clendening. The following month it was resolved 'that we cannot look on the present state to which our Poorhouse is now reduced, unable to supply them with food, often a supply of credit and unable from the state of the country to enforce payment of rates.' They laid the blame squarely on the shoulders of the Poor Law Commissioners. The final meeting of the Guardians took place on 11th August when the Board was dissolved and replaced by salaried Vice-Guardians.

George John, 3rd Marquis of Sligo, inherited the title at the age of 25 in the year the famine broke out. He was one of the principal landowners in the county and he had a seat in the House of Lords. It was to him that the people appealed when, on 31st August 1846, they marched through the town in an orderly body to Westport House and dropped to their knees before him. Lord Sligo was the Chairman of the Board of Guardians of Westport Union and also Westport Relief Committee. Together with two neighbouring landlords, Sir Robert Blosse and George Henry Moore, he chartered a vessel the Martha Washington that was loaded with 1,000 tons of flour in New Orleans and sailed for Westport where it arrived in June 1847. From there it was distributed at half-price to the distressed tenantry; Lord Sligo bore five-eights of the loss amounting to £3,012. Lord Sligo spoke out in the House of Lords and in letters to the London Times on behalf of the distressed tenantry and the failure of Government action. In letter to the Times on 17th December 1848 he accused the government of responsibility for the situation in Ireland stating that, in 1847, 26,000 people had been fed in the Westport Union and had been told to make no provision for the future:

'.... There are now therefore at this moment, in obedience to the law, 26,000 people in Westport who are destitute of food, fuel and clothing and the long account of money spent will not feed the crowds of destitute, the rates cannot, so it as if the Union be left to that fund alone then myriads must perish by famine.'

If the Famine spelt the end of the cottier class in rural Ireland, it also spelled the beginning of the end of the landlord class. Lord Sligo had a reputed income of £7,200 with outgoings of £6,000. The burden of the poor fell heavily on the landlord, not alone had they to pay the rate on their own land but also on any

Lord Sligo's Town House.

tenants with less than 4 acres. Lord Sligo was forced to borrow to pay the rates. He closed up Westport House and with his family went to live in a house in the town. A further problem as the famine progressed was the non-payment of rents, which eventually led him to consider evictions.

The clergy of the various denominations played a major role in the relief of the distressed. They were to the fore in the Relief Committees and acted as their eyes and ears. They made lists of the distressed families and distributed relief tickets. The Sisters of Mercy, who had recently come to the town, fed and educated the children in their schools and also helped out in the Workhouse. The various clergy also acted as chaplains in the Workhouse and on one day, having anointed 33 persons stricken with the fever, the R.C. chaplain next day found only 3 still alive. On 23rd August 1847 the R.C. Chaplain consecrated a patch of waste ground near the Workhouse, known locally as 'The Rocky' as a mass grave for those who died of the fever.

The Protestant Chaplin, the Rev. Patrick Pounden, The Secretary of Westport Relief Committee, was himself to die having contracted the fever.

*This article first appeared in **Cathair na Mart No. 4. (1984).***

AN OUTLINE HISTORY OF THE TOWN OF WESTPORT

PART V

GEORGE CLENDINING – BORN IN WESTPORT 1770 DIED IN WESTPORT 1843

George Clendining was born in Westport in the year 1770, the second son of the Rev. Alexander Clendining, Vicar of Westport. His father was a native of Co. Longford, who graduated from Trinity College Dublin in 1742 to the diocese of Killala, and he was later appointed to the incumbency of the parish of Aughavale (Oughabale), where he ministered for many years as Vicar of Westport, in the old parish church, which now lies in ruins beside the Carrowbeg River in the Demesne. In 1766 he married a local girl Eleanor Clarke of Carrowbeg. They had three sons, John George and Thomas Valentine, and two daughters, Mary and Elizabeth. They most probably resided in a house at the Octagon, which is listed in Lord Altamont's rent roll of 1785, and is adjacent to the old church via Church Street.

George was educated locally, and 1785 at the tender age of 15, entered Trinity College with his older brother John. He had not such a distinguished record in college as his brother who took an M.D. Degree, and is not recorded as having graduated. On leaving Trinity in 1788, George settled at home and held the position of Port Surveyor, a customs and excise appointment in the Custom House at Westport Quay. He was a regular churchgoer and attended vestry meetings. In 1790 he was elected a Church Warden, a position which he held for most of his life.

In 1792 he received a Commission of the Peace for Co. Mayo. This was a voluntary, unpaid, judicial appointment, which entitled him to sit on the Bench at Petty Sessions to hear minor cases such as would come before a district justice today. There were some ten local J.P.s in the Westport district, and they dispensed justice in the Petty Sessions house sitting on Thursdays at 1 p.m., where all summonses by individual magistrates were to be brought before the assembled Bench. J.P.s were also entitled to sit on the Bench at Quarter Sessions, at which the more serious cases were tried by judge and jury. Though this system has been replaced in the Republic, it still survives in the United Kingdom to the present day. Much of George's unpopularity may have resulted from his position as J.P., but it must be remembered that this was the system in time of peace of maintaining law and order. The powers of the J.P.s were limited and appeals could be brought to the higher courts.

Rear of Grove House, Clendining Residence.

The rebellion of 1798 and subsequent landing of French forces under General Humbert at Killala, followed by their defeat at Ballinamuck by Cornwallis, resulted in the appointment of Clendining as agent to John Denis Browne, third earl of Altamont. His predecessor in this office was the famous John Gibbons, Senior, who had played a prominent role in the organization of the United Irishmen in the district, and who was proscribed following the defeat at Ballinamuck. He was captured in 1799 but escaped to France, where he joined the Irish Legion and died in exile. His son 'Johnny the Rebel' held out in Connemara for many years until he was betrayed and publicly hanged in Westport. During the rebellion the Clendinings were regarded as loyalists, and the house and property were damaged, and wines, spirits, crops and clothing, were appropriated to the amount of £500.

George Clendining took up residence, following his appointment as agent, in the Gibbons property on Mill Street and became a close associate of Lord Altamont, whose property he administered. He also had close connections with the Moores of Moore Hall and the O'Donels of Newport House. He was a witness at the wedding of George Moore to Louisa Browne, which took place by special licence in Westport House in 1807, and one of his daughters was later to marry Sir Richard O'Donel, of Newport House. Their son, Sir George Clendining O'Donel, was the

last baronet of that name as he died without issue. The story is told that as a dowry, Clendining offered his daughter's weight in gold, and that for added value the daughter concealed two smoothing irons under her dress.
George married Margaret Nicolson, and their son John was born in 1798. He later entered Trinity College and graduated an M.D., establishing a practice in London. His other sons, George, Junior and Alexander, were also educated in Trinity College. Alexander acted as agent to the Moores of Moore Hall, and they both assisted in the merchant banking business established by their father. There were five daughters, one of whom met with a tragic accident on Monument Hill. Another married into the O'Donels of Newport House. After the death of the Rev. Alexander Clendining in 1799, George had the maintenance of his two sisters. His widowed mother Eleanor lived with her son Thomas Valentine at Thomastown, where she died in 1830, aged 84.

George Clendining was a self-made man. From the humble position of the family on their arrival in Westport, the vicar's son amassed a large personal fortune and became a person of great influence and social standing in the town of Westport. After his appointment as agent to Lord Altamont following 1798, he set up a merchant banking business, at a time when joint-stock banking was in its infancy, and at a time when the town of Westport was growing and developing as a centre of trade and industry with a thriving port. The Clendinings and other merchant families of the period, contributed to this rapid growth by their entrepreneurship and enterprise, and their names were household words in nineteenth century Westport. In 1826 Clendining was appointed Agent to the Bank of Ireland and established one of the earliest branches of the bank outside of Dublin. The requirements demanded by the governors were £10,000 on deposit with a further £10,000 in securities. The bank flourished, with offices on Mill Street, where George had built an imposing mansion to replace the Gibbons property. The building, in the Gothic style, is peculiar in that the front entrance faces Monument Hill and the rear fronts onto Mill Street.

Like all great men George Clendining was a controversial figure even in his own time, and he should only be judged by the standards of that age, and by a careful study of the records and documents of the time. His politics, religion and position, would have alienated him from the popular movements of the period. Yet he was respected by members of his own class, and was a well-known figure in the town of Westport. Unwanted infants were deposited on his doorstep, and those in need approached his door seeking 'charitable loans'. A writer to the Connaught Ranger, who witnessed the mail-coach travelling the length of the town to collect him and one of the proprietors of the other Castlebar newspaper Mayo Constitution, went on to ask "Who are these Clendinings that they should be entitled to such an unusual compliment?" The local press of the time were deeply involved in politics, the Constitution and Ranger supporting rival political opinions.

At the age of 73 and following a long illness, George Clendining died at his residence on Mill Street, Westport, on Thursday, 6 July, 1843. His remains were removed to the Church of Ireland (now in ruins in Westport Demesne) where for many years his father had ministered and where he himself had acted as a Church Warden. His funeral took place to Aughavale (Oughavale) Cemetery on Sunday 9 July, where his remains were interred in the family plot, to the east of the old church. The following is a contemporary account of these events, taken from the Connaught Ranger of 10 July 1843:

> ...At an early hour on Thursday morning in Westport after a protracted and exceedingly painful illness, borne with Christian resignation and becoming submission to the all-wise providence, George Clendining, Esq., aged 75 years, deeply and sincerely regretted by a numerous sorrow-circle of most attracted relations and friends. During the long period of Mr. Clendining's residence in Westport, he held a variety of important public situations, the confidential duties of which he discharged with unexcelled zeal, undoubted integrity and unflinching fidelity, commanding the respect and at the same time winning the devoted esteem of all who held commercial or monetary intercourse with him. Never was there a more affectionate father, indulgent husband, attracted brother, or thoroughly sincere friend, and the manner in which these attributes were generally appreciated was univocally testified yesterday, when one of the most respectful assemblages we ever witnessed, accompanied his mortal remains to the family burial place at Oughavale, gentle men of all creeds and political opinions giving audible expression to their heartfelt sorrow at his regretted demise. In Mr. Clendining the destitute and distressed people, not alone of Westport, but of the County at large found a liberal benefactor and they too, alas, will have sad reason for deploring his death.

On Monday, 10th July 1843, the day after his funeral, a requisition calling a public meeting for the purpose of erecting a suitable memorial to his memory, was signed by sixty-three persons of the county, and subsequently published in the Mayo Constitution.

> ...We, the undersigned, request a meeting of the friends of the late esteemed George Clendining, Esq., at the Hotel of Westport on Thursday, 20th July, at 12 o'clock, for the purpose of adopting the best means of erecting, in the town of Westport, a lasting testimonial to the memory of that venerated gentleman. Westport, 10th July, 1843 (Signed):
>
> | | |
> |---|---|
> | Sligo | H. Blake, Lieut. Co., J.P. |
> | Altamont | James Smyth |
> | James de Burgh Browne | P. Pounden, Rector, Westport. |
> | (9th Lancer) | |
> | Peter Browne | Fitzgerald Higgins, J.P. |

J.D. Browne	B. Burke, R.C. Dean, P.P.
Richard Levingston	James Pinkerton
Samuel O'Malley, Bart.	Geo. Gildea, Rector, Newport
Andrew C. Lynch, J.P., D.L.	CourtneyKenny, J.P.
George H. Moore, D.L.	A. Thompson, Maj. Gen., J.P.
Owen O'Malley, J.P., D.L.,	Graham Acton, M.D.
J.C. Garvey, J.P.	James Cuffe, J.P.
Wm. Levingston.	George Ormsby, J.P.
Patrick C. Lynch, J.P.	Thomas Ormsby, J.P.
George Acton	Thomas Elwood, J.P.
R.W. McIlree, J.P.	W. H. Parker, J.P.
Joseph Burke, J.P.	H. Waldron, J.P.
Benjamin Jennings, J.P.	Robert Eprins
J.J. Stewart, J.P.	Matthew Gibbons
Robert Fair, J.P.	Thomas H. Bourke
Theobald Burke, J.P.	John F. Bourke
Edward Deane, J.P.	M. MacDonnell, J.P.
Dominic J. Burke, J.P.	Joseph Myles MacDonnell
R. Buchannan, J.P.	Peter Tuohy
D. J. Cruise, R.M.	Ignatius Kelly, Jn.
John Burke, Ballinew	Patrick Boyd
J. Dillon, M.D.	St. Clair O'Malley
C. J. MacDonnell	Charles O'Malley, Q.C.
W.W. Graham	Patrick Hamilton, M.D.
James Hamilton, Clk	Pierce George Barron
Peter Burke, M.D.	John C. Larmine
Richard Dawsley, Col.	William Larmine
Francis Burke, M.D.	Thomas Gallogly
George Hildebrand	A. Bole

On 28 July, 1843, the Mayo Constitution reported as follows:
Testimonial to the late George Clendining, Esq.:
Pursuant to the aforementioned requisition a numerous meeting of the friends of the justly esteemed and venerated gentlemen was held in Robinson's (now the Railway Hotel) Hotel. Westport on Thursday, 20th July, at 12 o'clock, where the following resolutions were adopted and subscriptions to a considerable amount entered into.

John Browne, Esq., of Mount Browne in the chair. Proposed by Capt. F.G. Higgins and seconded by William Levingston, Esq., that Dr. Dillion be asked to act as secretary.

Proposed by R.W. McIlree, Esq. and seconded by J.T.S. Stewart, Esq., that W. M. Patton, Esq. Be asked to act as treasurer.
Proposed by Richard Levingston and seconded by M. MacDonnell, Esq., W. M. Patton Esq. Be asked to act as treasurer.

Proposed by Richard Levingston and seconded by M. MacDonnell, Esq., Resolved – That our admiration of the character of George Clendining and our sincere sorrow for his death, and only equalled by our anxiety to perpetuate his memory amongst us by the erection of a Public Testimonial, that will hand down to posterity the strongest and most enduring expression of our feeling.
Proposed by Major O'Malley and seconded by J.C. Garvey, Esq., Resolved – That a Public Testimonial worth of his memory be erected in such a place in the town of Westport, as shall be approved by the lord of the soil and by the committee appointed to carry our wishes into effect.
Proposed by Capt. F.G. Higgins and seconded by W. Levingston, Esq., Resolved – That a committee not exceeding 15 be appointed to carry out the object of this meeting, consisting of the Earl of Altamont, the chairman, the treasurer, the secretary, the movers and seconders of resolutions, and that others be named by them.

The following gentlemen were named as the committee:

Earl of Altamont	John c. Garvey Esq.,
John Browne Esq., Mountbrowne	William Levingston, Esq.,
Richard Levingston, Esq.	M. MacDonnell, Esq.,
Major O'Malley	Rev. George R. Gildea
Capt. F.G. Higgins	T.T.S. Steward, Esq.
Rev. P. Pounden, Rector	W.M. Patton, Esq. (Treasurer)
Very Rev. Dean Burke, P.P.	F. Burke, Esq., M.D.
James Pinkerton, Esq.	T. Dillon, Esq., (Secretary)

Resolved – That the 1st meeting of the Committee shall take place on Monday, 31st July, at 12 o'clock in the dining room of the Grand Jury, Courthouse, Castlebar.
(Signed)   John Browne   Chairman
               J. Dillon   Secretary

Proposed by J.C. Garvey, Esq., and seconded by Major O'Malley, Resolved– That Mr. Browne do leave the chair and that Mr. Pounden be called there to.
Resolved – That the thanks of the meeting be given to Mr. Browne for the efficient and dignified conduct of the meeting.
(Signed)   P. Pounden   Chairman
               J. Dillon   Secretary

Clendining Monument (Postcard in Clew Bay Heritage Centre)

The monument was erected as a result of the above meeting on the eve of the famine. It consisted of a full length statue of Clendining on a column, over an octagonal podium, with two female figures sitting on the podium, representing his benevolence and philanthropy, one clutching a young child. The Clendining coat-of-arms was rendered on two sides facing Shop Street and the Market House. The inscription 'To the memory of George Clendining' faced James's Street and Peter Street, and the inscription 'Born in Westport 1770, died in Westport 1843' was on the remaining four sides. The monument was an imposing one for a provincial town, as can be seen from the Laurence print of circa 1910.

From the date of its erection (circa 1845), this monument has been the subject of controversy. As early as 1853 it is reported by Sir John Forbes, a visitor to the town, that there are those who even now, prognosticate the precipitation of his effigy, one of those days, from its present lofty position.

In 1990 the figure of Saint Patrick, sculpted by Ken Thompson, was erected. Scenes from the saint's life were incorporated into the panels on the plinth. (Ed.)

His figure was used for target practice by Free State troops billeted in the Town Hall in 1923-4, when his head was shot off. Finally the end came in 1943 – the centenary of his death – when the Urban Council were debating a motion on the removal of Queen Victoria's statue from outside Leinster House. They decided that they would also remove the statues, crests and inscriptions, from the monument. Their remains are now at the Clew Bay Heritage Centre.

There have been a number of proposals down the years as to what should be done with what remains of the monument. Christ the King was proposed in the 1940s, St. Patrick in the 1950s, Major John MacBride in the 1960s. An Foras Forbartha in their Urban design study in the 1970s recommended a full restoration of the monument as it was. Now in 1985, the present Urban Council are taking up the matter, and are seeking advice from interested parties with a view to a partial restoration.

This article first appeared in ***Cathair na Mart No. 5. (1985).***

APPENDIX 1.

Voters List Prepared for Election to Grattan's Parliament in 1783 from the Estate of the Earl of Altamont.

(The spellings are as in the old records).

Submitted by **John Mayock.**

Owen O'Malley, Rosbeg.
Randal McDonnell.
Matt Sterling, Ballinvoy and Aughagower.
James Blake, Gurtrencanny.
Wm. Huston, South Mall.
Thomas Tempster, South Mall.
George Brown, Ballinock.
Thomas Jackson, Tuarbuck.
James Smith, Tuarbuck.
Patrick Ormsby, Tuarbuck.
Hon. G. Browne, Moyne.
Robert James, Tubberaune.
Alexander Reed, Tawney Park, Knappainine.
Anthony Bohanan, Tubbernane.
Alexander Clendening, High St.
James Gaughan, Bridge Street.
Thomas Gerard, Bridge Street.
John Clark, Mill St.
Edward Huston, Roughane, Kilkil.
Valentine Fitzgerald, Octagon.
Henny Duffrild, Sandy Hill.
Hon. H. Brown.
George Goss, Bridge St.
Thomas Jordan, Bridge St.
Daniel Lackey, Mill St.
Mick Kearns, Mill St.
Mick Needham, Mill St.
Robert Shaw, Bridge St.
Thomas Gaughan, Mill St.
James McAnally, Tubbernane.
Edward Devine, Bridge St.
Richard Walton, Mill St.
William Tackery, Bridge St.
Hon. John Brown, Killdavoggy.
Michael Buchanan, Tubberaune.
Hon. James Brown, Coolbarrack.
John Cornfield, Bridge St.
Dr. Lapworth, High St.
James Wallace, Bridge St.
John and Bartley Cornfield, Bridge St.
Thomas Little, High St.
Thomas Fitzgerald, Doonbrittan.
Ignatius Carter, High St.
John Leviston, Bridge St.
Hon. H. Brown, Glenumera.
Edward McGill, Bridge St.
John Barrett, Kingfisher Island.
Edmond Jordan, Kelsallagh.
Thomas Creeney, Deerintaggart.
John Clarke, Buckvary.
Jeremiah Davis, Furnace.
James and William Clark, Ardigommon.
Pat Stamford, Derrycroft.
Richard Baker, Bridge St.
Phil McLeane, Knockispricane.
James Dobbin, Knockispricane.
William and James Harwood, Bridge St.
William Bowen, High Street.

John Rock, Bridge St.
John Wilson, Knockunaslane.
John Parks, Tonranny.
Peter Brown, Octagon.
John Wilks, Knockispricane.
Thomas Fleming, Knockispricane.
Thomas Moore, Tawneypark, Knappamore.
David Davis, Knappamore.
Thomas Davis, Knappamore.
David A. Gildea, Kilkill.
Moses Morris, Kilkill.
Francis Higgins, Kilkill.
John Northford, Carrownalorgan.
James Davis, Shop St.
Elizabeth and Geoffrey Bourke, Letterkehane.
James Wilson, Knappamore Davis.
Richard Maberry, Kilkill.
John Pierce, Knappamore.
Laurence McBride, Bridge St.
Ignatius Charles James Lynagh, Gowl and Mahana.
Joseph Lambert, Drissleane.
James Dixon, Ballinacarriga.
William Noone, Buckwaria.
Sam Wilson, Knappamore.
William Jordan, Inishmall Island.
Robertson Liveston, Tonranny.
Nicolo Peretti, Fresh Water Bath.
Thomas Wilson, Tonranny.
Thomas Arthur, Tonranny.
John Marshel, Tonranny.
William Stephens, Tonranny.
Robert Hudson, Tonranny.
Robert McNab, Buckwaria.
Thomas McCausland, Buckwaria.
John Sandys, Buckwaria.
John Gallagher, Buckwaria.
Joseph Acton, Buckwaria.
James Tighe, Buckwaria.
John Collins, Buckwaria.
Wm. Atkinson, Ardygommon.
Thomas Brown, Ardygommon.
George Goss, Ardygommon.
Thomas Cosgrave, Knappaghmore.
James Blean, Knappaghmore.
George Bermingham, Fairhill.
David Bole, Tauney Park.
Robert Atkinson, Bridge St.
Richard Farrell, Bridge St.
Henry Piatt, Bridge St.
G. Sterling, Bridge St.
Henry Gale, Menur.
Robert McGill, Bridge St.
John Kelly, Bridge St.
Bart Tolster, Tuerbuck.
Thos. Reed, Tawney Park, Knappagh.
Andrew Bole, Tawney Park, Knappagh.
Thomas Cunnagh, Knappagh Davis.
James Blean, Knappagh Davis.
John Seymour, Pigeon Point.
Thomas Clark, Weaver.
John Clarke, 5th Dragoons, Weaver.
John Atkinson, - Breeches and Glove Maker.
John Bole, Knappagh Davis.
Robert Bole, Knappagh Cosgrave.
Edmond Kelly, Roslee.
Dan Kelly, Roslee.
John Kelly, Roslee.
James Fox, Creggawnagun.
John Cunningham, Batien Hill.
Richard Jones, Buckwaria.
Peter Toole, Buckwaria.
John Harewood, Buckwaria.
Archibald Cameron, Buckwaria.
Thomas Jordan, Touranly.
H. Hilderbrand, Cloonbanon.

APPENDIX 2.

A Topographical Dictionary of Ireland by Samuel Lewis (1837)

WESTPORT, a sea-port, market and post-town, in the parish of AUGHAVAL, barony of MURRISK, county of MAYO, and province of CONNAUGHT, 8½ miles (W.) from Castlebar, at the termination of the road from Dublin; containing 4448 inhabitants. This town is situated at the south-eastern extremity of Clew bay, and at the mouth of a small river, which falls into that portion of it constituting the bay or harbour of Westport. It is of modern date, and consists of three principal streets, and a Mall of large and handsome houses on both sides of the river, the banks of which are planted with trees and afford a pleasing promenade. The total number of houses is 617, most of which are well built and roofed with slate; a spacious and handsome hotel has been erected and splendidly furnished at the expense of the Marquess of Sligo, who assigns it rent-free to the landlord.

The approach from Castlebar is singularly beautiful, being enriched with the plantations of the Marquess of Sligo, and commanding a fine view of the mountain of Croaghpatrick, the lofty ranges of Achill and Erris terminating in the stupendous mountain of Nephin, and of Clew bay studded with innumerable picturesque islands. Westport House, the elegant mansion of the Marquess, who is proprietor of the town, and to which is an entrance from the Mall, is a handsome and spacious structure of hewn freestone, situated on the margin of a small lake in the surrounding demesne, which is also embellished with the windings of the Westport river, on which are two picturesque waterfalls; it commands some beautiful views of the bay, with its islands and shipping. Near the town are also Murrisk Abbey, the seat of J. Garvey, Esq.; Marino, of J. Cuff, Esq.; and Trafalgar Lodge, of C. Higgins, Esq.

The trade of the port, which is of comparatively recent origin, consists in the exportation of agricultural produce, particularly corn, and in the importation of timber from America and the Baltic, and of articles of British manufacture. In the year 1834, 116,117 quarters of grain and 5140 cwts. of flour and meal were shipped hence for different ports in England and Scotland. The number of vessels registered as belonging to the port, in that year, was 6, of the aggregate burden of 123 tons; 4 foreign vessels and 97 from British ports entered inwards, and one foreign vessel and 153 to British ports cleared outwards, in the same year.

The herring fishery is still carried on here, though not so extensively as in 1780, when the port was first established for its use; the number of boats employed and the quantity of fish taken vary considerably.
The port is advantageously situated for trade at the head of Clew bay, which is 8 miles in breadth and from 10 to 12 in length, and has two entrances, one on the north and another on the south of Clare island, which occupies about a third part of the mouth of the bay, and on which a lighthouse has been erected. The ordinary channel leading into the bay or harbour of Westport is that of Beulascrona, which is marked out by a small lighthouse on the northern beach, erected by the corporation for improving the port of Dublin; and also by a light erected by the Marquess of Sligo. The entrance is 240 fathoms wide and 6 fathoms deep; but there are shoals on each side, extending on the north from 200 to 300 fathoms (N. W. by W.) of the light; and on the south, or Doreinnis side,

nearly half a mile in the same direction seaward; but the intermediate channel is clear (S. E. by E.). When within the entrance, a vessel may anchor anywhere behind the bar of stones on the south side, called Doreinnis, in two fathoms or less, which is the ordinary place for vessels trading to Westport; or turning round the eastern end of the isle, a vessel may enter the harbour of Innis Gort, which is completely sheltered on all sides, and anchor in from three to five fathoms; or passing the entrance to Innis Gort, may anchor behind an island on the left, called Innis Lyre, in two fathoms or less.

From Innis Lyre up to the quays at Westport, buoys are placed along the channel, a distance of three miles: vessels drawing 13 feet of water can come up to the quays, where the spring tides rise to the height of 14 and neap to 8 feet. The quays are now being extended, and when completed will be nearly a mile in length. A commodious range of warehouses and stores has been built for the merchants of the town, and ranging with them are the king's stores, a neat building but less extensive. The custom-house is well arranged; the amount of duties paid in 1836 was £577. 8. 4.

In the town is an extensive distillery belonging to W. Livingston, Esq., established in 1826, producing annually about 60,000 gallons of whiskey and consuming 9000 bushels of grain; a brewery belonging to the same gentleman, and established by his father in 1800, has very much declined since the reduction of the duty on spirits, but is still considerable; in both these concerns about 150 men are regularly employed. Another brewery, with a malting concern, has been established by Messrs. Graham, who have two salt-works and three corn-stores on the quay, and a tannery in the town, affording together employment to 30 persons, and to double that number during the winter. The Manor flour and oatmeal-mills were built in 1808, and are set in motion by two water-wheels equal in power to 30 horses. At Belclare is a cotton factory, in which are 26 looms, affording employment to 30 men and a considerable number of women and children.

About two miles from the town are the bleach-green and linen and cotton-manufactory of Messrs. Pinkerton and Thompson, in which are 24 power-looms, producing weekly 48 webs of 52 yards each, and affording constant employment to 50, and when in full operation to more than 200, men. The market is on Thursday; and fairs are held on Jan. 1st, May 25th, Aug. 6th, and Dec. 1st.

A chief constabulary police force is stationed in the town, which is also the head of the coast-guard district, comprising the stations of Innisturk, Old Head, Islandmore, Mynish, Achilbeg, and Keem, and including a force of 6 officers and 52 men, under the control of a resident inspecting commander. The general sessions for the county are held here annually in April, and petty sessions every Thursday; a manorial court is also held on the last Friday in every month, at which debts not exceeding £10 Irish are recoverable. The court-house is a neat and well-adapted building; there are also a good market-house and a linen-hall.

The parish church is situated within the demesne of the Marquess of Sligo; and on the Mall is a handsome R. C. chapel, erected in 1820 by Dr. Kelly, at an expense of £6000; the altar is embellished with a fine painting of the Crucifixion. There are also places of worship for Presbyterians in connection with the Synod of Ulster, of the third class, and for Wesleyan Methodists. On the estate of Mr. Garvey are some interesting remains of the ancient abbey of Murrisk, founded by the O'Malleys, lords of this country.

BOOKS FOR SALE

Back issues of Cathair na Mart No.13 (1993) to No.32 (2014) are available at €10 each. Cheques should be made payable to Westport Historical Society. Payment can also be made online at *www.westportheritage.com*
Cathair na Mart No.33 (2016) is no longer available. Articles from this journal may be downloaded from *www.westport1916.com*

Síle Uí Mhaoluaidh (Ed.), **Father Manus Sweeney, a Mayo Priest in the Rebellion of 1798.** €20 (rare).
Liam Bane, **The Bishop in Politics, Life and Career of John MacEvilly** €25 (rare).
Pronsias Ó Maolmhuaidh, **Athair na hAthbheochana.** €30. (rare).
Michael Brady, **A Sailors Story.** €5.00.
Guide to the Clew Bay Archaeological Trail. €10.
Soccer History, Westport United 1911-2011. €20.

Postage and packing per item –
Ireland €4; Great Britain €6; Europe €6: U.S.A. €7.
FREE p&p on orders over €50.

Apply to the **Clew Bay Heritage Centre, The Quay, Westport, Co. Mayo, Ireland.**
Email : *westportheritage@eircom.net*

The editor thanks the following for their assistance in the preparation of this journal, Ann Ludden, Brónach Joyce, Sal O'Connor.

Design and Layout by **Michelle Gannon – Eye in the Clock,** Westport

HON. EDITOR: AIDEN CLARKE, ROSBEG, WESTPORT, CO.MAYO.

While every care is taken with the publishing of the material in this journal, the editor cannot be held responsible for the opinions expressed by the authors, or for any errors of fact. Contributions are welcome and should be typewritten on CD (Microsoft Word), or as an email attachment and accompanied by biographical details of the authors and relevant illustrations in uncompressed jpg. format.

Made in the USA
Columbia, SC
06 September 2018